Proverbs 3:

ROCK BOTTOM

THE HEROIN ADDICT NEXT DOOR

Alex,
I praying 2019
is your best year
ever!

Sincerely,

Rocky

ROCK BOTTOM

THE HEROIN ADDICT NEXT DOOR

BY ROCKY ROMANO

an imprint of the Armory Publishing Group, LLC

Rock Bottom: The Heroin Addict Next Door
by Rocky Romano

The Armory Publishing Group, including all its imprints, is committed to publishing works of quality and integrity. In that spirit, we are proud to offer this book to our readers; however, the story, the experiences, and the words are the author's alone. The conversations in the book all come from the author's recollections, though they are not written to represent word-for-word transcripts. Rather, the author has retold them in a way that evokes the feeling and meaning of what was said and in all instances, the essence of the dialogue is accurate.

ISBN: 978-1-947051-01-0 (paperback)
ISBN: 978-1-947051-00-3 (ebook)

Library of Congress Control Number: 2017940664

Published by Lion's Share Books, an imprint of the Armory Publishing Group, LLC. Littleton, Colorado, USA. www.ArmoryPublishing.com
For bulk purchases of this book, please email info@armorypublishing.com.

Edited by Doug Kehr and Denise Wynn
Interior Design by Armory Publishing Group
Cover Design by Armory Publishing Group
Cover Photo by Danny Dodge

Printed in the United States of America

TABLE OF CONTENTS

*This book is dedicated to my lovely wife, Tamara.
She knows the bondage and suffering of addiction as well
as the beauty of sobriety. She inspires all who know her
and her smile is like a lighthouse to my soul.*

*This also is for those struggling with addiction and
their family members. In a very real way,
for everyone involved, it's the fight of their life.*

*If this book saves one life,
it has achieved its intended purpose.*

*With Love,
Rocky Romano*

INTRODUCTION

Being an addict just plain sucks. Reflecting back on my journey, I see now what a powerful stronghold addiction had on my mind, body, and spirit. A wise person once said to me, "If you have to control your drinking or using, it is already out of control!" For me it took hitting "rock bottom" before I realized I was out of control.

More than anything else, I want my story to bring hope to those struggling with an addiction or who have loved ones who are fighting their own battles.

I've spoken to many kids over the past few years and have asked them a simple question: What do you want to be when you grow up? Believe it or not, not one has ever said they wanted to be a drug addict or alcoholic. Zero, nada, zip, not one!

You don't have to be a statistician to realize that various forms of addiction have risen steadily over the past two decades. Do a quick Google search and you'll see numbers that say there are over 17 million alcoholics in the United States, not counting those who are functional alcoholics and binge drinkers. One estimate states that 23.9 million Americans 12 years of age and older have used illicit or prescription drugs.[1] That makes it a staggering 40.9 million Americans dependent upon alcohol or drugs!

The problem is real. This is the story of my journey from how I lost everything because of my addiction to how I became clean.

I wouldn't wish for anyone to go through what I went through, but I know they will, which is why I'm sharing my story. Now that I am on this side of the misery, I am actually thankful for my experience.

I pray that my story will offer encouragement to those who are on a downward spiral and to their families. Know that there is hope!

---

[1] "New US Survey: 23.9 Million Aged 12 or Older Were Drug Users." Workers' Compensation Institute. September 5, 2013. Accessed December 21, 2016. http://www.wci360.com/news/article/new-us-survey-23.9-million-aged-12-or-older-were-drug-users.

THE ACCIDENTAL ADDICT

I didn't plan to be an addict.

No addict ever plans to become addicted.

My plan was to squeeze every possible drop of fun out of life as I maneuvered my way up the ladder—to collect the toys, make some noise, and to die rich and happy. And I hoped along the way to maybe, just maybe, prove something to myself and others.

But become an addict? That wasn't on the agenda...right up until the moment I couldn't take it *off* the agenda.

If you've never been addicted, you might not understand how an addiction—any addiction—slowly consumes your daily life, strangling your ability to see past whatever substance you crave. You've never rolled out of bed with just one thought gnawing at you: *How do I get more?*

Addictions are a hunger—a hunger that may grow subtly or come crashing into your life ready to swallow you whole. Addicts find themselves spinning out of control, preoccupied with whatever substance temporarily levels them out and lets them function. No matter the consequences, an addict focuses on short-term gratification, with no concern for the long-term cost.

If you've never been addicted, you can only imagine a life like that.

It's a life I lived.

No one really has a handle yet on what addiction really is and exactly what causes it. Some studies have documented the connection between learning processes and addiction for decades. Through research, neuroscientists are starting to recognize which brain regions are involved in addictive behaviors.

A key agent for addiction in these regions is the neurotransmitter dopamine, a chemical that increases with sex, drugs, and rock and roll. I don't know the science behind it, but somehow it is associated with many pleasurable experiences.

For me, heroin provided a sense of comfort and love that I never experienced from people, and I began believing I couldn't survive without it. I'm not a professional, but I know what I like.

Professionals use the word "addiction" several ways.

Sometimes the word is all about biology. It describes how a human body begins to tolerate a substance like heroin or alcohol, effectively requiring more and more of the substance to achieve the same effect. Stop the drug cold turkey and an addict experiences physical and psychological withdrawal symptoms which are—trust me—not something you'd enjoy. But continually raising the intake of a drug leads to even worse outcomes.

Addiction squeezes a person between two options—both of which can cripple or kill. Quit or continue.

Sometimes "addiction" describes compulsions that aren't substance-related. Think porn, food, sex, gambling, shopping, video games, and even social media.

The moment a behavior crosses the line and becomes an unhealthy preoccupation that's pursued no matter what impact it has on a person's health, mental state, or social relationships —that's an addiction.

Experts even debate whether addiction is a disease or a mental illness. There's no consensus on whether it's nature or nurture or the result of genetics or social and psychological factors.

Frankly, I don't care, and here's why: No matter how an addiction enters your life, it's devastating. It will crumple you up and kick you to the curb.

An addiction can literally end your life—as it nearly ended mine.

I'll tell you right from the start I'm not a psychologist.

I'm an addict—or at least I was one—and I've worked with hundreds of other addicts. There's not a story, an excuse, or a plea for help I've not heard at least once from someone whose life was falling apart. I've heard it all and at one time or another, and even said most of it.

But I survived. And I survived *heroin*—a bear trap of a drug that few escape without scars.

If you're an addict, I'm not writing to lecture you. I'm writing to help save your life.

And if you're someone who loves an addict—or whose heart has been broken by an addict—I'm writing to try and help you understand. To crawl inside that life long enough to see out through an addict's eyes.

That's why I'm writing. I thought you should know.

Rock Bottom is my story and, like most stories, it will best make sense if I start at the beginning.

2

SON OF MY FATHER

Let me tell you about my dad.

Charles Pasquale Romano was old school in every sense of the word. As you may have guessed, he was raised in one of those big Italian families that are supposed to be gathered around a kitchen table heaped high with lasagna and love.

Those aren't the cards that were dealt to my dad. He came up hard in and around Minneapolis, a poor kid in a poor family that dished out more beatings than bruschetta.

My father landed in foster care, bouncing between homes whenever his temper got the best of him, which happened often. Because fighting came naturally to him, my father found his way to a gym where he climbed into the boxing ring to learn a trade. He was good—good enough to work his way up the ranks until he finally was earning a living unleashing flurries of lefts, rights, and uppercuts that sent other men to the mat, bruised and bloody.

The life of a boxer fit him—and it wasn't until Uncle Sam called him into the army to fight the Germans in World War II that he laid down his gloves.

My father didn't talk much about his childhood—such as it was—or the War. What I know is that in France a bomb detonated near his transport truck. He was injured and lost some of his hearing *and* his ability to make a living in the ring.

What he didn't lose was his taste for violence.

I know because long after my father was mustered out of the army, and moved to southern California to work for Bob's Big Boy restaurants, he still sometimes settled conflicts with his kids the way he knew best: with his fists. And when an old prizefighter tosses punches to make his point, it's memorable.

My dad married once before he met my mom, and had four children with which to hone his parenting skills: Roxy, Sharon, Mike, and John.

AND SON OF MY MOTHER

My mother, Joan, was born in China. Her father worked for the British government and was stationed in Shanghai when my mom was born. Unlike my dad, she was brought up in an affluent environment, which included butlers and servants to cater to their every need.

All of that took a nasty turn for the worse when the Japanese invaded China in 1939. She and her parents were thrown into a concentration camp and had all of their possessions confiscated. Hers was a true riches to rags story.

The camp was crowded, dirty, and food was scarce. For years she experienced the pain of hunger. She'd tell stories about dreaming of her favorite food only to wake up starving. She got me to watch the movie "Empire of the Sun" with her and said that was a good depiction of what she experienced.

She didn't, however, tell me *all* of her past tales. I found out as an adult that after the war my mom had married an American bisexual she had met in the concentration camp! Shortly after they married they settled in California. That marriage was short-lived; they divorced within a year.

Divorce would become a way of life for my mom.

Later in life I discovered they had a son they named Doug. The first time I met him, I was thirty-five years old.

My mom met another man and became Mrs. Bruce Conner of San Fernando Valley. That marriage didn't last long either, just long enough to have three additional children: Don, Fred, and Shelly.

LOVE AT FIRST FIGHT

My mom and dad met after they'd both been single for a while, and they decided to give marriage another try. Seven children soon became eight with the addition of Rocco "Rocky" Romano on a warm day in August of 1960. I was born in beautiful downtown Burbank, California and grew up loving the outdoors and playing any sport that involved a ball.

At just nine years old, I entered the "Ford Punt, Pass, and Kick" competition at the LA Coliseum and came in second for my age group. I remember telling my parents that the next year I would win. Which I did! I was so excited to get home to show my parents my trophy that I ran into the house shouting, "I won! I won!"

My joy was short lived. My parents told me that winning was great, but they had something more important to tell me. They told me that they were getting a divorce—effective immediately. Talk about getting the wind knocked out of your sails.

My mom had already packed and would take me with her to her best friend Jackie's house. We went to Jackie and Lee's house a lot growing up, and they had two kids: Lee Jr. and Alex, who were both my buddies. There were plenty of sleepovers and our parents were good friends. Maybe more than just "good friends."

OUT WITH THE OLD

It seems my mom and Lee had been having an affair and she was moving in with him and his two sons, bringing me along for the ride.

Goodbye Jackie, hello Joan and Rocky.

I was devastated. They say kids are resilient and divorce isn't a big deal, but I was left with a hole in my soul and in a state of total confusion. Lee was a man I liked, but now I saw him as the cause of my parents' divorce and I hated him for it. But mom was still my mom and I wanted to be with her.

My father decided to move to Reno, Nevada, and tried to convince me that moving with him would be my best option. It also was an opportunity for him to deny my mom all that he could. Over time, I realized I was just a pawn in their game of trying to hurt one another. Dad bribed me with a couple of LA Dodger games showing me how much fun we would have together, and it worked. I chose to move with him to Reno.

Life in Reno was good for a few years. I continued to play baseball and was the first player selected to make the Nevada Little League All-Star team. I even hit the game-winning home run to advance our team to the eighth round of the Little League World Series. I was only twelve years old, but was considered one of the best baseball players in the country for my age group. Recruiters were even starting to take notice.

I immersed myself totally into sports to try and ease the pain of my parents' divorce. At least all that garbage was behind me and now there was some stability. Or so I thought.

IN WITH THE NEW

My father met a French lady named Gigi, she worked in a casino. He became infatuated with her. Unfortunately for me, she didn't like children and gave him an ultimatum. Either I left or she left, his choice.

"It's my last chance for love," he told me, and he was going to take it.

You'd think that by this point I'd be at peace with disappointment, but that is a never-ending well and there was plenty left for me to experience.

Shortly after I turned fifteen, my dad loaded me, and all my belongings, in his car and drove us from Reno to North Hollywood, California, where my mom was living with Lee. Not a lot was said in the car and I wasn't sure what to expect. I hadn't seen my mom since we left for Reno years before.

When we arrived, my dad unloaded all of my stuff on the sidewalk, mumbled a terse goodbye, and drove off. As I stood there on the sidewalk the realization came over me that my own father had just abandoned me.

I gazed at the gate of my mom's triplex and didn't even know if she was expecting me. Never in my life had I experienced such sadness. A beating would have felt much better than I did in that moment.

Here lived a mother I didn't really know, staying with her best friend's ex-husband and his sons. And they would soon have a new roommate. I picked up my two bags and walked through the gate, up to the front door, and rang the doorbell.

Luckily, my mom was home and answered the door. She greeted me with a huge smile and seemed genuinely excited to see me. Obviously, she was expecting me. Dad had done something right.

She invited me in and there was Lee, the man that I'd grown to hate. He welcomed me into his home and let me settle in for a week or so before he laid down the law about his house rules. I wasn't sure what the future held for me; I just wanted to get through high school and then get out on my own.

THE NEW KID IN TOWN

Transferring from a high school in Reno, with all of 1,200 students, to a North Hollywood school with over 4,000 students crowding the halls was a cataclysmic shock. Overnight I went from strutting around campus, a first-string athlete and class leader, to being a *nobody*. Worse yet, it seemed that nobody even *wanted* to get to know me.

I can still remember that first week, and the torture of sitting out by the baseball field at lunch, eating alone. Shuffling to class, nodding to kids who just looked through me. I quickly sank into depression. So, after waiting what seemed like an eternity for someone to notice me, I did what I'd done all my life: I tried out for, and made, the baseball team. Then, the football and track teams as well.

Making friends among my teammates became much easier and by my senior year I was back in the popularity saddle once again, riding high. I was even voted "Class Flirt" alongside my female counterpart, a pretty girl named Penny—every boy's dream. But even then I knew I was just filling my time, staying busy, doing my best to bury the pain that had brought me to a new school, a new life.

Only later did I discover that I could run from the pain but I couldn't hide.

NO PLACE LIKE HOME

As good as my life was in school, it was equally as bad at home. My mom and stepdad would drink every night when they got home from work.

Every night.

Most of the time they would drink until they were drunk, and my stepbrother, J.R., and I would lie in our beds and listen to them curse and yell at each other until they passed out or went to bed. In the morning, they would get up, still hung-over, and act like nothing had happened. Then, they'd be off to work, and home again, only to repeat the cycle.

To his credit, my stepdad was a brilliant man who worked hard. He taught J.R. and I about how important it was to have a solid work ethic. He would insist we work hard in school and get good grades—*or else*. He even helped us with our homework if we needed it. His attention, however, was based entirely on performance. I can remember just one sporting event Lee Sr. attended. It was a football game in which I got hurt on the second play. I don't recall either him or my mom ever showing up for any other game.

Hard work and performance weren't the only lessons he taught us. The real lesson he taught us was how to get by in life as a functioning alcoholic.

Finally, I graduated from North Hollywood in 1978 and took a job stocking shelves in a grocery store. Not glamorous, but it kept me busy until I would start school at L.A. Valley College. I'd landed a football scholarship.

But I got injured.

All the sudden, sports—that place I'd always found friends and success—was now a closed book.

"At least I was out on my own," I thought.

Like so many high school graduates, I didn't have a clue as to what I wanted to do with my life. I had survived a painful childhood and was looking forward to being my own boss and doing what I wanted to do. That is of course, *if* I could figure out what that was.

THE DOWNHILL SLIDE

Without the anchor of sports, I attended college off and on and had no definitive career plan. As a result, I rotated through a stack of short-term jobs, but nothing that lasted very long. Finally, I landed in the grocery business—buying and selling for a large retail chain. It was a solid job and after seven or eight years, still without a college degree, an opportunity presented itself. I was approached by a wine wholesaler to become a chain-store merchandise representative.

This job was my first break at trying to make a real living for myself, and the money was good. I jumped at the chance! Being in sales fit my personality to a tee. I like people and I like to talk, and I especially liked the potential income I could make.

My new goal was to buy a house. So, when I was 25, I moved back in with my mother and saved as much money as I could for a down payment. My mom's only stipulation was that I give her my paychecks. She deposited them into an account and gave me an allowance to live on.

Life was good, and even on my allowance I enjoyed the finer things in life. I especially began to like fine wines. After all, I had learned to drink hard and work hard from the best.

While vacationing in Puerto Vallarta several years later I met a beautiful woman from Mexico City, her name was Nerea. What a woman! Nerea had beautiful dark hair, deep brown eyes, and to say I was smitten was a *huge* understatement.

She came from a wealthy family and had never learned to cook or clean, but who cared? Her smile did me in. When I spoke I couldn't complete a sentence without stuttering. We fell in love. But long distance relationships are difficult at best. We spoke on the phone at least once a week and every few months I flew down to Mexico for a visit.

During my second visit I proposed to Nerea, but she insisted I ask her father for permission. His family was from the northern part of Spain, also known as Basque Country, which in English must be translated as, "We grow them large."

Nerea's father, Felix, stood 6'3" and weighed about 300 pounds. He said "yes"—reluctantly.

Having done my part, I left it to Nerea and her family to plan the wedding of all weddings. They rented the entire town of Tepozitlan, a picturesque spot about forty-five minutes from Mexico City—some 400 people showed up.

After the wedding, we bought a condo in Canyon Country, California. My bride was able to find employment as a graphic artist while I continued to work for the same liquor and wine distributor. In hindsight, it wasn't the best industry for me—a functioning alcoholic—to be in.

In 1994 we had a son and called him Andoni—a chip off the old Romano block. I thought, *"Now I have the opportunity to be the father I never had."* But, I didn't know where to start.

I couldn't wait till the years I'd get to teach him how to throw a ball and ride a bike. But, little did I know, my plans were about to crash and burn.

ADIOS NEREA

Nerea wanted to be a stay-at-home mom and quit her job. To make up for the loss of income, I needed to get more involved at work. It was during this time my addiction to alcohol began to rear its ugly head.

Unfortunately for me, Nerea didn't share in my love for booze, so she devised a clever plan to get herself back to Mexico with our son. She told me she wanted to take a three-week vacation to Mexico, so her parents could see Andoni, who was just three years old at the time.

A week after she went to Mexico, Nerea called me at work and said she needed to see me. I told her I'd fly out as soon as I could, but she then informed me she was already in Denver with her best friend. I was shocked. She then told me to meet her at an Olive Garden Restaurant in Westminster, Colorado, at 5 p.m. that evening. I met her at the restaurant while Christina waited in their rental car, knowing I was about to receive some bad news. *At least the food was Italian.*

Over breadsticks Nerea told me she wanted a divorce, effective immediately. I guess the divorce apple doesn't fall too far from the Romano tree. She even left our son in Mexico with her parents, so I wouldn't have any chance of custody. I also wouldn't have the chance of being the father that I hoped I would be.

It felt like I'd been sucker-punched in the gut and dredged up all the old feelings and emotions I had when my dad dropped me off in California to live with my mom.

Abandoned.

Rejected.

Unwanted.

Alone.

My self-esteem had left only to be substituted with condemnation. These feelings came crashing in on me like a tidal wave roaring in my ears. She tried to discuss the more pragmatic issues of divorce; visitation rights, settlement of property, and a little thing called alimony. She might as well have been talking to the waiter, since my attention was focused on my crushed and broken heart.

The night ended when we settled on something she had written down on a legal pad to give to her lawyer and she said she was headed back to Mexico. I can barely remember what the settlement was, and I couldn't care less if I had anything. My world had collapsed and I didn't know where to turn.

HATCHET BURYING 101

A few days later, still in shock and reeling from a crushed spirit, I stood across the street at my neighbor Ed's house and watched Nerea instruct the movers as they loaded up the last few items into the moving truck. After a while the truck was full, but they weren't able to find enough room for the refrigerator. My soon-to-be ex-wife had me buy the refrigerator back from her for $300 before she drove off. All she left me with was a bed, a TV, and that darn fridge.

Turning to Ed, I said, "I have nothing left." He reminded me that all the items being taken away were just *stuff* and that I would fill the house back up in no time at all.

In my mind, I believed that burying the hatchet was simply my choice to forgive and move on. The problem was that I couldn't forget. The pain that I felt constantly reminded me of those old feelings of unworthiness, and abandonment. I couldn't move on with my life because I couldn't forget the pain of Nerea leaving me and taking my son.

And the nightmare was only just beginning.

When Nerea left me she wasn't a citizen and didn't seem to have an interest in becoming one. I thought I'd probably never hear from her again after the divorce was finalized. She came. She saw. She conquered. And then, she returned home. End of story.

What a surprise when, eight years later, I *did* hear from her. She wanted half of the equity that I had built in my house during the years she'd been gone. Still feeling responsible for my son, I offered her $30,000 cash, about half of the equity that the house had acquired. She summarily rejected that offer and hired an attorney who had family connections high up in the government.

The lawyer came after me hard and because of something to do with NAFTA, she was able to get *$40,000*. Later, I found out that by the time she paid her lawyer's fees, she only received $14,000, which was $16,000 *less* than my original offer. On top of that, I had to pay a lawyer $30,000 to defend myself.

During that time, I was able to fly to Mexico City twice to see my son, but he was never allowed to see me in the United States. The original court settlement of our divorce stipulated that I would pay her $1,200 a month in child support, and that I would receive visitation rights for Andoni to come and see me every summer and a holiday that Nerea and I agreed to every other year. She decided not to live up to her end of the agreement, so I tried to pursue a case in Mexico to uphold my visitation rights. I discovered that the pendulum of NAFTA does not swing both ways.

Frustrated with the system and situation, I felt that my only recourse was to stop paying alimony. So I stopped and felt incredibly guilty because I knew I had a responsibility to my son. I never did learn how to bury the hatchet and simply move on. The pain of loss and unforgiveness etched their scars deeper on my heart.

Maybe if I concentrated on my career, everything would work out all right...

WORK IS GOOD FOR THE SOUL...AND POCKET

Work. I knew how to work. I poured myself into my job and did well—better than well. Soon, I was promoted to the position of on-premise manager for a large beverage company.

With the new job, I was able to remodel my home and fulfilling Ed's prophecy, I filled it to the brim with brand new furniture and *stuff*. I'd never lost my taste for the finer things, and that extended to beautiful cars. I bought an exquisite classic 1986 Porsche Carrera that was so sweet I entered it into local car shows.

Several years went by and I was offered a position as the Southwest Sales Manager for a Sonoma Winery. With more responsibility came more salary and perks, including a company car, and an exorbitant expense account. Following the path of happiness offered in the American Dream, I upgraded to a 6,800 square foot home with a million dollar view located just off the 18th green at an exclusive country club. I was beginning to acquire all the things in life that should make a person happy: a new house, a new Lexus, a new Jeep, a classic Porsche, three new motorcycles, and even a new girlfriend. Life could not get any better, right? Wrong. I was never more miserable.

Then things took another ugly turn.

BE LIKE MIKE

For the many years I worked in the wine business I hung out with Mike, a guy I met at a local gym. My best friend, George, had always warned me about Mike. His warnings were particularly about Mike's *more than recreational* drug use. Over the course of the decade that I knew Mike, his abuse got worse and worse.

And now my life was about to take a turn in the same direction.

One day, I found out through my girlfriend's son that his mom had found a new boyfriend. *Ouch*. I didn't see that coming at all. I moved out and let her keep the house and mortgage. She threw my stuff in the garage and I sold most of it.

Trying to move on, and still having money coming in, I quickly found a model home in a new subdivision that I liked and ordered one to be built for me. In the meantime, my buddy

Mike offered to let me move in with him and his wife while I was having the new home built.

Shortly after that, my mother was diagnosed with breast cancer. She fought a hard battle, but succumbed to this insidious disease. I didn't expect that, either.

My older half-brother, Alex, had recently died after a long and hard battle with alcoholism. I guess bad news really does come in threes. Everything seemed to be crashing in on me once again.

One night I told Mike about the pain I was experiencing—how much it hurt to feel *abandoned* and *worthless*. I felt like I was in a deep, dark pit with no chance of working my way out. My life was without purpose or meaning, and the despair I felt just kept getting more and more intense.

Mike then offered to let me try some of his OxyContin to ease the pain. Since it was a prescription drug, a medicine, I felt it would be OK to take it. I mean, *"It's legal, right?"*

He gave me a few lessons on the proper method for getting high fast on Oxy. The first time I snorted it I threw up, but the pain I was feeling was mitigated for a while—mission accomplished.

Since OxyContin was a prescription drug, Mike could only get as much as his prescription allowed. Once the prescription ran out, we needed to find another source. This introduced me to the dark world of drug dealers. Daily runs to meet his dealer became commonplace and his dealer soon became *my* dealer.

After a week, I was hooked.

The exorbitant cost of buying pharmaceutical drugs soon opened the door to buying illegal drugs, which were both cheaper and more powerful—the best of both worlds for an addict. I was introduced to what quickly became my favorite drug of choice, *heroin*. It was cheap, effective, and easy to obtain. This was the start of my downward spiral, one that would continue until I hit rock bottom.

To top it off, the winery I'd been working for fired me without any warning. This happened right after I ordered a brand new fresh-from-the-factory Porsche 911 Carrera. I'd saved some cash, but not enough for a new home, a new car, *and* a new drug habit. Depressed and alone, I wasn't sure what to do.

Of course, Mike was there to help ease the pain. Then again, my buddy Mike was having his own issues with abuse. I woke up one night and went down to the kitchen to get something to munch on. In the kitchen I saw Mike just standing there, as if in a trace, holding three open and melting ice cream containers. I knew Mike had a tolerance for drugs. He could take enough to kill an elephant, or at least a very large farm animal, and still function. Yet there he stood—paralyzed.

Later on I found out that he'd taken twenty-five, 80-milligram tablets of OxyContin, which is nothing more than pharmaceutical-grade heroin. Mike was so out of it, he couldn't even eat the ice cream. This should have been a warning for me about what effects drugs can have, but I was willing to do anything to numb the pain I was experiencing. *"Besides,"* I thought to myself, *"I'll never get as out of control as Mike."*

THE VOICE

After living with Mike and his wife for a while, the winery finally tracked me down and picked up the company car. I didn't like how my life was going, so I decided to get away for a while.

A Harley-Davidson Sportster would help me solve my problems…so I went out and bought a new one.

One day I was heading out to Denver International Airport to meet someone. I was doing about 75 miles an hour heading east on I-70. I needed to change lanes and checked my rear view mirror and saw it was all clear, when all of a sudden I heard a voice shout, "No!" so I stayed in my lane. A second later a BMW 525 passed me like I was standing still, doing well over 100 miles an hour. If I would have tried to change lanes I have no doubt I would have been killed.

Where did the voice come from? Was I hallucinating? Did it come from a *higher power*? Was God trying to get my attention or protect me for some reason?

I was never much of a religious person. Even if there was a God, I assumed He must not have cared very much about me. I had no idea where that voice came from, nor did I care very much.

The reality was that I was unemployed and needed more and more cash to feed my growing habit. A few days later I sold the Harley for pennies on the dollar.

THE FALL

When my home was completed, I moved out of Mike's house. I bought a new Toyota Camry to get around until my new Porsche arrived. But my hunger for heroin kept getting worse and I quickly depleted my remaining cash stockpile. After 17 years in Colorado, I was going to lose everything I'd worked so hard to acquire, all because of my growing heroin addiction.

One of the first things to go was my brand new and beloved Porsche that I had just recently picked up. I guess missing payments to support my drug habit just didn't sit well with the bank. They found a very persistent and clever repo man to find me.

For three weeks or so, I was able to stay a step or two ahead of him, but the repo man must have done his homework. One Thursday evening he waited until I snuck my car into the garage and after I got out of my car, I saw a tow truck slowly make its way down the narrow alley. He finally got me.

Without a job I needed to come up with some way to support my heroin addiction. I began selling anything of value that I had in my home—furniture, tools, knick-knacks—anything to feed the habit. When that stuff began to run out, I started doing things I never thought I would ever do.

Desperate times called for desperate actions and my need for heroin certainly made me desperate. I'd walk into Walmart stores and go to the tool section, take some tools, and just walk out of the door, setting off alarms in the process. Then, I'd jump in my car and drive off to the nearest pawn shop to get as much money as I could to feed the addiction.

As screwed up as my childhood was, it was instilled in me at an early age that it was wrong to steal. So, doing what I was doing just increased my feeling of guilt. I never dreamed I'd ever do such a thing. *So why did I?* Did I not have enough will power? Or did I just really lack moral principles?

The answer, as twisted as it was, was pretty simple. For me, my addiction eased the deep-down pain of not *being* or *feeling* loved.   Even when I was successful from a worldly perspective, I still had a sense of worthlessness and was willing to do anything to numb that pain. The result was that my addiction fed on itself.

The more I took, the more I needed. There was something going on in my brain that craved more of the pleasure and power I felt when high. And when I wasn't high, my sense of joylessness was overwhelming. The problem was that I needed more and more heroin to get the same effect. So I needed more and more money to feed my habit. Consequently, my life of crime continued to escalate.

I was finally arrested at a local Sam's Club on my second attempt to steal a DVD player. Because it was a misdemeanor theft, they only wrote me a ticket and let me go. *Thank God I didn't have to go jail and detox.* But I knew it was just a matter of time before I ended up in prison.

By this time, the bank also decided that since I wasn't making my mortgage payments, my new house that I'd been in less than a year would be repossessed. The good news was they offered to pay me a little over $2,000 cash if I could clear out by August 1st. And cash is a good incentive for a struggling heroin addict. This money would also provide what I needed to start over somewhere else.

California seemed like the best option for me since I still had some contacts there. I could also visit my half brother, Fred, in Las Vegas on the way there.

This new plan might actually be what I needed to get my act together.

CALIFORNIA OR BUST(ED)

I still had my 2005 Toyota Camry for the journey. Unfortunately, I was a little behind in its payments as well—OK, *a lot* behind. It was just a matter of time before another clever repo man picked up my last form of transportation.

But, that car was my ride to California, so I needed to keep it. There was a huge Park-n-Ride garage about a mile and a half or so from my house. I stowed it there. No way would anyone be able to find that particular car in a maze of hundreds of vehicles. This would keep the car safe while I cleaned up the house and collected the incentive money.

Around six o'clock in the evening, the day before I met a real estate agent to turn over my house keys, I drove the car back to my house so I could load it up with my remaining possessions before leaving town.

I had time for some heroin-influenced reflection on my life during that drive. Things didn't look good and I could feel the anxiety gnawing at me as I cautiously pulled into the garage and closed the door. I loaded the trunk and back seat with whatever I hadn't sold: clothes (including a dozen expensive custom suits), shoes, artwork, and toiletries. It took just forty-five minutes to put everything I owned in the Toyota.

Now I just needed to get the car back to the parking garage and walk home, so I could meet the real estate agent, get my check, and leave. Sweating and paranoid, I opened the garage door, expecting to see the repo guy and his tow truck. All clear —so off I sped to the Park-n-Ride.

That mile and a half journey seemed to take forever. Halfway there a sheriff's car passed me going the other way. I was sure he did a double take. I thought, *"Oh no, I'm finished and going to jail,"* but he kept on going. I finally made it to the garage and parked the car, locked it, and returned home to wait in that empty house until I could get the money and run. I was beginning to think that maybe everything would turn out OK.

THE DRIVE

Early the next morning, I woke up with the same old feelings of anxiousness. The drugs masked those feelings for a while, only to have them return with a vengeance. I pressed forward with the plan. The real estate agent showed up and walked through the home. He declared it was clean enough to release me from my obligation. He even rounded up and gave me a check for $2,100.

I was now ready to start my journey.

Before I left to pick up my car, a sympathetic friend stopped by and gave me seven Suboxone tablets—a drug used to treat adults who are dependent on opioid drugs like the ones I was addicted to. They were to help me calm my nerves and ease the withdrawal symptoms of heroin that I would experience during the long drive out to California.

The best way to describe withdrawal symptoms from heroin addiction is like having the worst case of flu you have ever had, then, multiply that by a thousand.

After taking a couple of Suboxone tablets, I left Denver around 11 a.m. headed for Las Vegas to spend some time with my half brother, Fred. When I got on I-70 heading west I became overcome with paranoia and had a panic attack. I just *knew* that the repo man was on my tail and would soon overtake me and leave me with nothing.

Paralyzed with fear, coming down off of heroin, and fueled by Suboxone, I thought that if I could just make it to the Utah border everything would be OK. I don't remember much else about that journey, but I do remember seeing the "Welcome to Utah" sign, and breathing a sigh of genuine relief. Everything would be fine *now*.

About halfway through Utah, I needed to rest and decided to get a room. I pulled into a Motel 6 knowing it was time for another Suboxone to relax my mind and body, so I could get to sleep. Tomorrow would be a new day, and it would have to be better than the day I'd just had.

Again, I awoke in the early morning to the all-too-familiar sickening effects of heroin withdrawals. I have told people I would rather fight ten guys in a dark alley than face the withdrawal of heroin. It's an ongoing battle that makes you wish you were dead. And, in the moment, there's no relief in sight (except more drugs to mask the agonizing effects).

I took another Suboxone and started off to Las Vegas.

After being on the road for several uncomfortable hours, I happened to see a liquor store. Liquor stores in Utah are more rare than an Italian at a bar mitzvah, so I pulled in to get something to numb the pain. They sold 1.75 liter bottles, which should be more than enough to medicate myself until I arrived in Las Vegas.

Freshly supplied, I poured some whiskey in my coffee cup as soon as I got back in the car, thinking I could pace myself and just take the edge off a bit. The hours droned by and on more than one occasion I started to drift off behind the wheel. I struggled to focus on the road, sky, or anything to somehow stay awake. I kept drifting off, but didn't want to stop. It was Las Vegas or die trying.

SIN CITY

Bum, bum, bum...bum, bum, bum. With a jerk, I awoke from my catatonic stupor by the sound of the safety ridges on the side of the road. I was doing 80 miles per hour and heading for the soft gravel shoulder and a serious end. Now I was wide-awake.

The adrenaline rush stayed with me for another hour or so and then I went back to the bottle. There was only an hour and a half left to my destination, so I filled my mug half full—*over* and *over* and *over* again.

To this day I do not remember driving into Las Vegas.

When I woke up, I was parked under an awning in an apartment complex. There was a tapping on my window, and when I came a little to my senses, I realized the tapping came from a police officer. I rolled down the window and the officer told me the apartment manager had called the cops and asked them to remove "a vagrant who was parked in his apartment complex with a car that was filled with stuff."

The officer at first wanted to book me and take me off to jail for public intoxication. I convinced him that I was privately sleeping off being drunk, and certainly didn't want to drive anywhere in that condition, so I found a place I thought would be safe to drink and then sleep it off. There are *some* advantages to being a smooth talking salesman.

Something I said must have convinced him that it would be OK for me to call my half brother, Fred, to see if he'd come claim me and move my car. Not quite the introduction to Fred that I was planning. When Fred arrived I could tell he was excited to see me, but disappointed at my drunken state.

Fred moved my car and all of my worldly possessions to a public parking lot and then came back and picked me up. He drove me to his apartment and we talked a while before it was time to go to bed. *"Maybe things would be better in the morning,"* I thought.

The next day brought more of the same pain—the incredible discomfort from heroin withdrawal—and this time I had no Suboxone to help. There was a corner convenience store across from Fred's apartment that I hoped would have something for relief. I headed to the store and found a four-pack of wine that might help take the edge off my pain and suffering. It helped briefly but like always, I came back to the pain of my reality. After two days with my half brother, I knew it was time to move on.

This time, I headed for Bodfish, California, an hour-and-a half east of Bakersfield. There I planned to stay with another of my mom's former husbands, Paul. He was her husband when she died. I believe she'd finally found true love and her marriage to Paul lasted sixteen years.

I had a good relationship with Paul and I knew he would take me in.

BODFISH

Paul welcomed me with open arms and an open liquor cabinet. He enabled me to substitute my heroin addiction with even more alcohol than I'd been used to. Booze was his addiction of choice.

At least alcohol wouldn't be as dangerous and deadly as heroin, right?

Paul and I were a pair made in heaven, or hell, depending on how you were counting. With him being retired and me being unemployed, we had plenty of time to drink. And drink. And drink some more. We stayed buzzed most of the time.

We got drunk in the morning and stayed that way until we went to bed. Then we repeated the same routine the next day. In between binges, I tried to get a job in town but had no luck.

The drinking eased the pain I was feeling, and even brought me out of my depression, at least for a while. But alcohol actually makes depression *worse*. It impairs your thinking, and you can't make that connection so it's easy to believe if a little alcohol helps, then more has got to be better.

Depressed, I elevated my drinking to new heights. But the more I drank, the more depressed I became. After hitting it hard for a couple of days and consuming two half-gallon bottles of Jim Beam, I started to have serious thoughts about suicide. I felt trapped, like a caged animal, with absolutely no hope and no place to go.

Life stunk and I couldn't handle it any longer.

IF AT FIRST YOU DON'T SUCCEED

The next morning, I got up and started the day as I usually did—with a drink. My stepdad, Paul, had to run into town on some errand and left me all alone in his house.

Sitting on the couch I saw one of his hunting rifles leaning against the wall. I got up and walked over to it. Depressed and armed with the courage of alcohol, I started to look for bullets. I found them in a drawer nearby and took one out of the box.

Grabbing the rifle and bullet I went back to the chair and sat down. I thought, *"I can end all the pain I'm feeling—right now. Right here."* Loading the bullet into the chamber, I put the butt of the gun at my feet and put the barrel in my mouth. I took a deep breath and pulled the trigger.

Click. The gun didn't fire!

What are the chances of that happening? I've never heard of anyone who's had a misfire in a modern rifle with modern bullets. Shocked at the misfire and stunned that I couldn't even kill myself, I put the gun back and poured myself another drink.

After two days of non-stop drinking, my stepdad had to leave again for the day. I decided that I would try once again to end my miserable existence.

41

This time, I decided I'd use a tried and true method: I'd cut my wrists and bleed out. I found some old-school double-edge razor blades in the guest bathroom medicine cabinet. I sat in the living room and cut deep into both wrists and also my left leg.

Drunk and bleeding, the phone rang and for some reason I answered it. It was my stepbrother, JR, who lived in Monterey, California. He immediately knew I didn't sound right and asked me what was wrong. I told him I'd been helping Paul and had fallen off the roof and cut myself, but I'd be OK. We said our goodbyes, but fifteen minutes later he called back, and by that time I was slipping into unconsciousness and couldn't answer the phone.

He later told me the Holy Spirit told him to call an ambulance, which he did. He told them where I was, but the ambulance couldn't find the house and called my brother back to get better directions. By the time they arrived, thirty minutes later, I was unconscious and close to death.

After breaking the front door down, they found me on the floor in the living room and tried to stabilize my condition. They loaded me into the ambulance for the ride to the hospital, but because of the seriousness of my condition, they called the Medivac helicopter. It came and took me to the hospital in Bakersfield.

The hospital trauma team sewed up my wounds and replenished my blood supply. To this day I'm not exactly sure what all happened. However, because I didn't have any insurance, they discharged me at 2 a.m. with nothing but the pair of bloody shorts that I came in with and a hospital nightgown top. Fortunately, I had some cash in my pocket and was able to find a cab to take me to the closest cheap motel.

The next morning, still groggy from the ordeal, I figured I had just enough money for some breakfast and to buy a pair of flip-flops.

Little did I know whom I'd meet next...

DEEPER INTO DARKNESS

Walking out of the cheap motel room wearing only a hospital gown and shorts is no way to greet the day. But, for some reason, I was still alive. As I squinted at the bright morning sun through bloodshot eyes, twisting one way and then the next to stretch the sleep out of my tired bones, I noticed someone dressed nearly as badly as me. A homeless woman.

If I had to guess, she was probably in her early 50's, but it was hard to tell. There's something about being homeless, dealing with the worry and circumstances of having no place to call your own, that ages a person. She could have been 50, or 40, maybe even younger. The miles she'd traveled had worn her down—but she hadn't lost her edge.

Peering out from under a mop of brown hair were two piercing bluish-green eyes. Those eyes could see right through you and I've never forgotten when she turned them on me. She spoke first.

"I know you," she said, studying my face. "I saw you last night. They saved you didn't they?"

Even the fog of alcohol couldn't keep my questions from forming. How did she know? Had she been at the hospital? Was she just guessing? Did she think I was someone else?

She was pushing a shopping cart filled to the brim with a big black trash bag packed with her possessions. She certainly hadn't covered the ten miles between the hospital and this motel parking lot pushing it. In the end, I didn't know what to say, so I just smiled and asked for something.

"Excuse me ma'am, but would you happen to have a shirt in your bag that I might be able to wear?" I didn't have too much to lose by asking her.

"As a matter of fact, I might," she responded. She opened her bag and, rummaging around, she at last pulled out a white shirt. She handed it to me with a mischievous smile.

Across the front of the shirt, in big red letters was written, "Angels."

I pulled on the shirt and invited her to have breakfast with me at a greasy spoon next to the motel. She agreed and parked her cart next to a window so that she could keep an eye on it while we went inside.

We ordered breakfast and spent the next 20 minutes talking. Really, it was more like me talking while she ravenously consumed everything in sight. I mean everything, including what was left on my plate. I wasn't too hungry after my ordeal.

After breakfast she followed me over to the motel's parking lot. I was anxious to get on with my day and figure out how I'd get back to Paul's house in Bodfish.

Without much enthusiasm I asked, "What are you doing today?"

She answered, "A minister of the Gospel is going to pick me up today!"

I was half listening because I was checking my pockets to see how much money I had left. When I looked up—she was *gone*. Her *and* her shopping cart.

Had I hallucinated the whole thing? Blacked out? I was mystified, yet, there I stood with an "Angels" shirt and a lot of questions.

How does a homeless woman watch me get wheeled into an emergency room at a hospital ten miles away the night before, meet me at an out-of-way motel, give me an "Angels" shirt, and then just disappear?

Was she an angel?

In the seventy-two hours leading up to that moment, my miserable life had been saved—*twice*—and then I'd encountered this woman. You'd think this might be a wake up call. Maybe it was time for a change. But first I needed to get in touch with Paul so he could take me back to his place—and let him know I was still alive.

TIME FOR A CHANGE

My stepdad was worried about me. When he got home that evening, he saw the front door broken in and blood everywhere. He thought it might have been the scene of a murder. Calling the authorities in Bodfish didn't help because I was in Bakersfield, so nobody could give him any news about me or about what happened.

When I finally called him, he was glad I was alive, but I knew I'd worn out my welcome. He drove over and picked me up and as we talked I realized I'd become more than a minor interruption and inconvenience in his life. I helped clean up his place and he graciously offered me an old motor home to stay in—but that would require me to pay rent somewhere to park it and I still didn't have a job or any prospects of one.

The other option was to call my stepbrother JR who'd actually saved my life. It was partly his "fault" I was still around anyway, so I figured he owed me. I called JR and told him I was a little down on my luck and needed a place to stay.

At this point, JR had no idea how much I was drinking and that I'd tried to commit suicide twice. I lied, and told him that I had fallen off the roof and landed on the steps, and some exposed nails cut me up pretty badly. All I knew is that I needed to recover. He said he'd check with his wife, Vicki, and see what she said.

The next day, he called back and said I could move in with them for a while. This was an opportunity for a fresh start. I could leave one thousand miles of wreckage and mess behind me. The day after that, I packed my Toyota to leave. Paul was concerned about my future, which looked dismal at best, but I'd become a big burden to him.

We said our goodbyes and I took off. I left for Monterrey, completely detoxed from heroin, but still a bit shaky from all the alcohol I'd consumed the past few weeks. On the drive, I had a lot of time to think about my life and what a mess it had become and how much I had lost. It felt like a dark cloud hovered over my vehicle all the way to Monterey. But the clouds broke as a sense that things might turn out all right after I got to JR's beautiful home over-looking Monterey Bay.

Maybe, just *maybe*, there was a light at the end of this dark tunnel of life that I had been traveling.

INTO THE DARKNESS

Wrapped in a bear hug, JR and I embraced warmly in the driveway right after I arrived. It was such a good feeling because it had been more than a decade since I had last seen him. His wife, Vicki, was another story. She had a smile on her face when she saw me, but I could tell there was apprehension in her heart. Since they'd become committed Christians, they felt moved to help me, but they also knew I'd be a challenge. To honor the chance they were giving me, I determined to try with all my strength not to let them down.

We immediately went to lunch and talked about the years gone by. While we consumed a few alcoholic beverages, I expanded on my recent battle with heroin. I even reiterated the lie that I had fallen off Paul's roof and ended up in the Bakersfield hospital.

It took a while, but I finally landed a temporary job a few weeks later. I was hired to help the owner of a custom lighting shop in downtown Monterey who was going out of business and needed help liquidating his inventory. I was in my element. I felt like I could sell anything to anyone.

After working there a couple of weeks, I met a woman who had come in to buy some discounted lighting. We hit it off and I asked her out and we started dating. She was quite the party animal and *not* what the doctor ordered. She liked to drink—a lot. And I joined in. I felt I had my drinking under control though, and after my temporary job was over, I was ready for a real job.

That came less than a month later when I landed a great six-figure job as a territory sales manager with a company that sold powered mobility devices to doctors. The company immediately flew me to Texas for two weeks of training. By this time, I was completely detoxed from heroin and had remained fairly sober for a month or so—at least during the day.

In the evenings, alone in a hotel room, my old friend depression paid me a visit. Four days into the training, I decided to see the company doctor and tell him I had some back pain and needed something to control it so I could work. I am still amazed at how easy it was to get prescriptions for pain medication. Maybe because I was such a good salesman and liar, I had no problem selling my pain. For a little while, at least.

MY OLD FRIEND

I made it through the two weeks of training, but the prescription I got was enough to wake up the sleeping giant known as addiction. When I returned home I continued to get scripts of Vicodin, first going to one doctor and then another. It didn't take long for the insurance company to catch on to my tricks, and they notified the doctors to not write me any more prescriptions.

Again I started going through detox and became deeply uncomfortable. By this time, I had moved out of my stepbrother's house and into a converted garage on English Street. It was still in Monterey, only a few blocks from JR's house, but it was far removed from what I'd grown accustomed to. It was dark and depressing like me, so it kind of felt like I belonged there. JR later confided to me that when he first came into the apartment, he felt it had a spirit of oppression all over it.

The more discomfort I felt, the more dark and depressed I became. Alcohol called out to me.

One Saturday afternoon around 3 p.m. I succumbed to the temptation with a nice bottle of Pinot Noir. It soothed me like an old friend, which led to more drinking on Sunday. I got home from work Monday around 3 p.m. and started drinking again.

Within four weeks, I was drinking earlier and continuing later each day until I had to have a drink to wake up and one to fall asleep—and just about all the time in between. Obviously, it began to affect my work.

The great job that I'd landed came to a screeching halt when I stopped showing up for the mandatory 7 a.m. huddles. When confronted by one of the "big bosses" about why I hadn't been attending, I told him I was sick. In a sense, it was partially true—I was sick of my miserable existence—but the real reason was my alcohol abuse.

At this point, I didn't have any meaningful relationships in my life. No real friends, no girlfriends, I even avoided seeing JR because I didn't want him to know how much I was drinking.

It was me against the world…and the world was winning.

And then, I was fired. Again.

My world darkened even further.

BANKRUPTCY OF SPIRIT

I'll never forget looking into the mirror one morning and not recognizing the person in the reflection. The old Rocky

Romano had moved out and in his place was a dark and sinister shell of the person I had once been. Yet I still thought I could control how much alcohol I was consuming. I could quit anytime I wanted to quit—but *not until after the next drink.*

Luckily for me, the local gas station could sell me beer when they opened at 6 a.m., that helped me get by until it became time to get serious with my drinking.

One evening in a local Monterey bar, I got into a fight—something I was fairly good at. The owner of the bar said I could stay since I hadn't started the fight, and I think it was also because I was one of his best customers. I figured another drink or two would calm me down. On the way back to my dark hovel, I was pulled over by the Monterey police and received the first of three Driving Under the Influence violations.

The second DUI, I was so drunk I don't remember getting pulled over and going to jail. After I was released, I went back to my old and familiar habit and set the scene to receive my third DUI.

I drank all morning, which meant I needed to replenish my booze supply by driving to the local liquor store. Backing out of the parking lot, I backed right into a parked car, and since I was still a little buzzed, I left the scene of the accident immediately. Unfortunately for me, some bystanders saw what happened and were able to get my license plate number. They called the police. I was tracked down and thrown in jail once again. I was three for three—three DUI's in three weeks.

My life was spiraling out of control.

After getting out of jail, I'd pretty much hit rock bottom. I had three DUI's, one TKO in a bar fight, several major legal expenses, and I'd just about run out of money. *And*, added to all that, I'd just about run out of any hope that my life would ever be worth living.

My bankruptcy was so much more than financial, it extended to my mental, physical, and spiritual states.

One afternoon around 2 p.m., in my dark and oppressive studio apartment, I remember crying at my hopelessness. Sliding off the bed and falling to my knees, I cried out to a God I wasn't sure I believed in, but I had nowhere else to turn.

"God, if you're real, I need your help. I just can't do this any more. If you're who they say you are, please help me...please!"

That was the first real prayer I'd ever prayed. My heart was truly broken and contrite. I was ready to surrender and give it all up.

I'd tried to change in the past, or so I thought. It turns out that surrendering and feeling remorse aren't the same. Before I was married, I'd gotten involved with Alcoholic Anonymous and even had a sponsor, but I couldn't care less about a higher power. I just needed some direction because I knew I was drinking a little too much.

I remember my sponsor, Thad, telling me that what we were attempting to do was not working. He said it was probably because I was not yet ready to surrender and he actually stopped sponsoring me. When your AA sponsor quits on you, then you know things are bad.

But this time it really felt different.

I SEE THE LIGHT

I mmediately after I prayed that prayer in my dark and depressing hovel, I felt a strange sense of relief. I had a peace I'd never experienced before. It was weird.

Perhaps now was the time to get into an AA program again. Since I couldn't drive, I found one in downtown Monterey I could attend. I walked a few blocks to Del Monte Avenue to catch the 3 p.m. bus to downtown Monterey, and walked a short distance to the AA meeting. I was a little early, but I kind of knew what to expect. If you've never been to an AA meeting before, then you should know that you can't just slide into the room and find a place in the back row and be anonymous. *You know, like we do in church.*

"Anonymous" in Alcoholics Anonymous has nothing to do with being anonymous. There is no place—at least no place this side of a car dealership showroom, anyway—more welcoming than an AA meeting. Everyone there has shown up to soak in encouragement. To make connections for accountability. To walk out with one more relationship forged with someone who understands what it takes to be sober.

I was in the room for less than ten seconds before heads swiveled and I was introducing myself.

"My name is Rocky...and I'm an alcoholic." By that simple confession, it felt like some of the weight I had been carrying had been lifted off my shoulders. I even volunteered to share what was going on in my life. How helpless I felt. How out of control I was. How I was unable to change my situation through my own effort. I even told them about my prayer.

No one judged me. In fact, they welcomed me as one of their own. It was like having the family I'd never had. Maybe there was some help that would keep me from continuing in my self-destructive behavior.

What was that strange feeling I felt...was it *hope*?

A SHINING BEACON

Before I left the meeting I was approached by Suzette. She had a faith that emanated from her countenance like a beacon from a lighthouse.

"Hello. I heard you share and I want you to know I don't normally do this, but your story moved me. I work with the jails in Monterey and I have contacts in recovery circles. Here's my business card, and if you would like some help, please call me."

I told her that I didn't have any money and that I was in deep financial trouble.

"You don't need money, just call me if you would like some help," she said.

I took the bus back home and right after I walked into that tiny, dingy, studio apartment I called Suzette and said I needed help. She was true to her word and got me connected with some recovery groups.

My first interview was with New Life, a rehab center about a half-hour north of Monterey in Santa Cruz. JR drove me up there and we took a tour of the facility. It was very nice, but I didn't feel like that's where I was supposed to be. Suzette understood and said she'd continue to set up interviews with other recovery programs and added that, "…by God's grace the right opportunity would present itself."

She told me to be still and take it one day at a time. She later told me that she knew God had a plan for me. But even if I found a recovery program I liked, I still had little money and large legal problems. I decided to heed Suzette's advice and take it one day at a time.

Tomorrow I would go to another AA meeting and start looking for an attorney who might help me.

PAYING THE PIPER

The first four lawyers I called left me feeling depressed. They all wanted anywhere between $13,000 and $16,000 to handle the three DUI's.

I didn't have three dimes.

The fifth lawyer was named Shawn. I introduced myself and he asked me, "Who is this again?"

"Rocky Romano." I went on to explain my three DUI's and what it would cost to take care of those.

Maybe he could hear the disappointment and rejection in my voice, and after a slight hesitation, he asked me if I could get down to his office that very day. I asked him if an hour would be too soon. I quickly cleaned myself up, hopped on my bike, and was at his office an hour later.

He greeted me rather warmly for someone I had just met and took me into his private office.

"Sit down Rocky." He said it in a way that made me think we were old friends, and asked me what was going on.

I then proceeded to pour out my guts to this stranger as he intently listened. When I finished, he pointed to a note he'd placed under the glass that covered his massive wooden desk. It was from a very good friend of his who had died of alcoholism.

He then reached into his bottom desk drawer and pulled out a bottle of vodka. He explained that he keeps it there to remind him what killed his friend, who'd been sober for a very long time, but fell back into his destructive habit. He paused and then looked right at me, and said something I hadn't heard in a very long time.

"I believe in you, Rocky, and I know you can do this."

He then asked how much money I could scrape together. I told him I had around $500.

"I'll take it." He then asked what else I had—maybe a car?

I told him I had an old Lexus with 225,000 miles on it that had been given to me by a friend of my brother, JR.

"I'll take it," he said. He then told me that he'd take care of all my court appearances and that he believed God had a plan for my life that was way better than the plan I had.

I told him how grateful I was and that I was planning on entering a recovery program as soon as I could.

"That's great!" He seemed truly interested in my plans.

He said, "Come back tomorrow with the car, along with the title and keys. And don't forget the $500."

Looking back on this incident, I realize that he didn't need my $500 or the old Lexus; he was just making sure it cost me something. But when that's *all* you have, it really cost me everything. It was clear, I was going to have to be dependent on God for everything I had from then on.

THE ROAD TO RECOVERY

The next day, I had JR drop me and the car off at Shawn's office. Once again he greeted me warmly. I gave him the keys, title, and money and asked, "Now what?"

He told me he would take it from there and not to worry.

I hopped on the bus to take me back to the hovel.

Later that afternoon Suzette called. She told me about a place called Cityteam Ministries that was headquartered in San Jose, but had recovery programs in Oakland and San Francisco. She said they might be a good fit for me. I told her I was definitely interested.

The next day Suzette scheduled a phone interview for me to talk to the San Francisco recovery manager, Jonathan.

Jonathan was originally from Nagaland in East India, next to Myanmar. He sounded like he was speaking three languages at once, but every once in a while there was some English thrown in. If I really paid attention, I could make out what he was saying.

"Call back tomorrow," he said. There might be an opening for me in San Francisco or possibly Oakland. By the following day, he would know for sure.

That next day, we called and he said that there was an open bed in San Francisco and he would save it for me until the following week. However, he emphatically stated, my acceptance all depended upon me having a clean drug test when I arrived.

Things were beginning to move in a positive direction for me, which something I hadn't seen in a while. And then I did something I had never done before. I dropped to my knees and surrendered my life to Christ right then and there.

There were no missionaries at my door, no voices in my head, no heavenly chorus singing songs of praise, and no TV preachers telling me what to do.

It was just me and God.

It was surreal, almost like I was watching a movie of myself. I had never experienced anything like this during my days of addiction. Even in that dark, oppressive hovel, I felt genuine peace.

I couldn't wait to tell JR and Vicki that I had found a Christian recovery program and the Lord all on the same day because I knew they were still praying for me. When I asked them for a ride up to San Francisco, they were thrilled and offered to get some boxes and store my few possessions for the year I would be in the program.

We proceeded to pack up the studio dungeon on English Street, and while the apartment was the same, something was *different.* I felt good—no depression, no anxiety, no feeling of worthlessness, even though I had next to nothing.

I moved back in with JR and Vicki for the few days till it was time to go to the recovery program. Before leaving for San Francisco, I thought I would attend one last Monterey AA meeting with my new friends, and asked one of them to pick me up at JR's house. Waiting for my ride on a beautiful Monterey morning and enjoying the day, I got down on my knees again and cried out to God. I just plain felt good and wanted to thank Him for it.

Then, something unusual happened.

I SEE THE LIGHT

As soon as I finished praying the brightest light you could imagine flashed in front of my eyes, then immediately disappeared. When my sight returned, I looked around and expected to see if some one turned on a giant movie premiere light—like the one Commissioner Gordon used to call Batman.

I couldn't and still can't explain what happened.

There were no lights or lightning, or anything else around that could have caused that to happen.

As I was trying to understand what happened my friend showed up. He was a guy I recently met at Alcoholics Anonymous and was always happy to take me to meetings, even if I wasn't totally sober.

A year or so after I returned to Monterey from graduating from the recovery program, he recounted a story that I had no recollection of whatsoever.

He dropped me off at my hovel one evening after I attended an AA meeting totally inebriated. He told me to eat a banana, drink some water, and get some rest. He then left me all alone and went to his car to keep an eye on me.

It turns out that right after he left, I immediately jumped in my car and he followed me to the nearest liquor store. I got out of my car and two hoodlums attacked me right outside the liquor store. He told me that one of the guys hit me over the back of my head with an empty bottle and I went crazy. I laid both guys out cold. The owner of the shop called the police and when they arrived he testified that I was attacked and defended myself. I walked home while those two guys went to the hospital. That's how messed up I was most of the time. I'm probably glad I don't remember everything that I did while drunk.

Looking back I can see that God had been working in my life, and that I was no longer the same person whose first instinct was to fight my way out of things. I thank God for placing friends like him in my life to help me on the road to recovery. Maybe, just maybe, that light I just saw had something to do with God's presence in my life.

When my friend pulled up to take me to the meeting I was still in a state of euphoria. I was beginning to understand that God was calming my spirit and letting me know He is very real. What an incredible feeling that is, mere words cannot express what was going on inside me. Armed with this inner peace, I was looking forward to see what would happen at Cityteam in San Francisco.

7

CHANGING DIRECTIONS

The day before I was to leave for Cityteam, I got everything packed up. My brother came and we took my belongings to storage. Everything—and I mean *everything*—I now owned fit into these few boxes. I left for Cityteam with nothing, but the clothes on my back.

The excitement and anticipation of what the future held, not to mention my recently being *born again*, kept me looking forward. I still had no clue about what my future held or how things would unfold, but for once, I was okay with that.

JR and Vicki invited me for the proverbial "last supper" that evening, and during dinner I had that same peace about the future. As much as I enjoyed getting high, there is nothing that can compare to a genuine feeling of peace. It was more intoxicating than anything I had ever tried. After dinner, Vicki, volunteered to drive me up to San Francisco.

The next day we awoke to another beautiful Monterey morning and headed north. This new day brought new hope. The closer we got to our destination, the more the weight of what was happening began to overpower the peace I enjoyed. Was this what I was supposed to be doing? The excitement of new hope was being edged out by old fear.

The GPS instructed us to exit at 6th Street in San Francisco. This area is known as the TL, the Tenderloin District. It's an apt name because of what happens to you if you stay there too long—you get eaten alive like a piece of meat.

We exited on 6th Street and drove to Mission Street, made a u-turn, and stopped in front of our destination. I looked around and said a little desperate prayer: *Lord, everything seemed to be moving in the right direction, and You orchestrated everything according to Your will. What happened? I didn't ask you to send me to hell! Why am I here?*

Even Vicki had reservations about leaving me there and thought that this was not a good move for me. But there I was.

The best way to describe being dropped off in the Tenderloin is like a wounded animal being dropped off around a pack of hungry hyenas. The street was crawling with punks and pimps, addicts and alcoholics, hustlers and hookers, and it was just midday! I told Vicki to lock her doors, but to stick around until I got checked in. Slowly, I got out of the car. The air was thick with the smell of urine with just a hint of vomit. I made way through the graffiti-clad metal security gate in front of Cityteam Ministries. I was so freaked out by my surroundings I didn't see the doorbell and started pounding on the gate. One of the guys in the program heard me and came to the gate.

"Are you the parole officer?"

He knew I didn't fit in and I knew I didn't fit in. I was wearing the last vestiges of my worldly wardrobe; a Hawaiian shirt, designer blue jeans, and a pair of Johnston and Murphy loafers that would have made Don Johnson proud.

Quickly, I told him who I was and why I was there, and he took me to the recovery manager's office and told me to sit. Poor Vicki sat in the car all by herself, until I finally told him I needed to let her know that I was okay so she could go back home.

I ran out to her car and told her everything was fine, grabbed my bag, and gave her a goodbye hug. As she drove away, I saw her glance into her rearview mirror. That glance told me everything. She was filled with overwhelming apprehension about leaving me there. And she wasn't alone.

As Vicki drove off down Mission Street, those old feelings of abandonment came crawling back to the surface.

It could have been my dad in that car.

I was also flooded with an overwhelming sense of fear that I wanted to run away, but I took a deep breath and went back inside to wait. After 10 minutes or so, I was called into the office.

There to meet me were the Recovery Manager, Jonathan, and the house managers, Randy, and his buddy, Peter. I didn't know at the time, but when Jonathan was explaining the program to me, Randy and Peter were passing notes saying things like, "I give this guy a week, tops!"

Jonathan explained that Cityteam's program lasted one year, and that if I could stay sober on 6th Street, then I could stay sober anywhere. I told him that I was committed to the program and then they checked me in.

I asked the guy helping me where the bedrooms were and he just laughed. He told me that the new guys sleep on cots stored in the closet on the main floor, and after a few months, if we move up to another level in the program, we will graduate to a new room. The upgrade from a cot was a bunk bed with four guys to a room and we would get to share two bathrooms and one shower. With everyone else who lives on that floor.

This prospect did nothing to lower my anxiety level. I was wallowing in my self-pity, and felt I had nothing to give to Cityteam.

Boy, was I ever wrong.

THE PROGRAM, THE PEOPLE, AND THE PEACE

My first night at Cityteam Ministry we served about 150 homeless people a meal. And because I was the new guy, I got to wash the dishes, both for that night *and* for the next 90 nights.

Nothing in my jet setting, party-guy past as a wine salesman had prepared me for standing in a steamy kitchen up to my elbows in scalding water. Scraping plates, slamming cutlery in and out of an industrial washer, mopping floors—this was all new territory for me—and I hadn't even figured out yet where I'd get to unfold my cot that evening.

We served the homeless five nights a week, every week, and also spent time in the Bible. It wasn't a choice, it was part of the program. Cityteam Ministry (CTM) is based on three pillars: learning what's in the Bible, AA, and accountability.

Each guy at CTM had two accountability partners and I'm talking *accountability*. I had to report to both of them and it didn't surprise me when I found out they compared notes. These guys weren't playing games and if I was going to find my way out of addiction, I couldn't play games, either.

During my first week, I was introduced to the man who would become my spiritual mentor, Paul Chan from San Francisco. He came every week to teach Bible classes and to meet with me. There are no words to describe how helpful he was in my life.

Monday through Friday, we all rolled out of bed (or off our cots) and went to a Bible study. There were other classes and parts of the programs, all of which wrapped up about 3 p.m. Dinner for the guys at Cityteam was at 5:00, and we served the homeless from 6:00 to 7:00 p.m. Then it was clean up, an hour or two to relax, and lights out. When the next morning came, we'd to do it all again.

On Saturdays we started the day with a hot meal and the clothing room was opened to us. We could pick up the latest designer fashions or maybe someone's old hand-me-downs, usually the latter, but at least I had clean clothes. At noon we served lunch to the homeless and also offered them clothing. Volunteer doctors and nurses provided medical care. Another thing we did was wash the feet of the homeless, a humbling experience, especially for the new guys at Cityteam.

This program got me to do something I had never done before: it took my eyes off of myself and my problems, and helped me focus on others who were even less fortunate. This was a totally new experience for me.

Anyone who came to the mission we tried to help. This got me thinking about myself less, but not thinking less about myself. I was still so selfish. There's a real blessing in serving others that I'd never known or considered because I was so immersed in the "me first" mentality that's so prevalent in America. It was all about me all the time...right? *Wrong!*

Something amazing happens to a person when they are broken and then surrounded by godly people who pray fervently all of the time. My life was being transformed from the selfish person I once was into being truly concerned and loving toward others. That alone was a small miracle. Even more miraculous was what I saw daily: men and women who were operating through the power of the Holy Spirit and showing it by unconditionally loving others in their midst.

People at Cityteam were serious about their faith and lived like they believed the Bible was actually true. Some became not only my friends, but also mentors. One of these mentors was a woman named Shirley—a godlier person would be hard to find. Once she knew I was going to stick around, she called me into her office every few weeks to talk, share Jesus, and pray with and for me.

Another amazing lady I met was Trudy, a hard-core Army Chaplain who told me that she didn't even want to know my name until I had been there for thirty to forty-five days. I really did not like her very much at first, but I grew to love her over time and began to see that her inside was as soft as her tough-as-nails exterior was hard. I thought of her as an M&M: chocolate inside surrounded by a hard shell.

These people were showing me in word and deed what genuine followers of Jesus looked like. The effect was powerful. Something was beginning to shift in me. I was changing in ways I never thought possible.

One Wednesday night I was at a praise and worship service at Cornerstone Church in San Francisco. My good friend, Dave, and I were on our knees deep in worship. I heard a small voice in my spirit say, *"Rocky, if you knew the things that I have prepared after this life, you would worry for nothing in this life."*

If you are wondering, the answer is *no*. No I do not normally hear voices in my head. In fact, I'd be highly skeptical of anyone who told me that they were having intense revelations from God. It's harder, however, to write it off when it happens to you, when you're *sober*.

Whatever happened, it had a profound effect on my life. I really didn't worry about stuff as much as I used to. It was freeing and allowed me to begin to focus on other people.

Over time I took on new responsibilities at the ministry. I became the hospitality host, overseeing the kitchen and serving of the homeless. The job included me saying prayer before the evening meals.

Me, saying prayers, out loud, in front of others!

That might not sound like much, but I had never said a prayer out loud before a group of people before in my life. This wasn't just a job, but something I looked forward to. Each night we served, I went outside and greeted every hungry and homeless person in line. I don't know if it affected them, but it brought great joy into my life to serve them. I saw real people with real needs, not just lazy slackers who were trying to live off the system. Serving, and being served, brought me something I had been trying to obtain through my own selfish effort.

Joy.

Peace.

Purpose.

Around 3:30 p.m. one afternoon, I was sitting on the main floor of the mission looking out through the security screen. As I observed all of the chaos of the world outside, I felt the presence of God within me. That sense covered me like a warm blanket of pure *love*. And I realized that it is what I had been looking for my entire life. All I could say was, "Thank You Lord, thank You!" I finally felt the "peace that passes all understanding" the Bible talks about.

MINISTRY OPPORTUNITIES

As time went on, I began to take on more ministry responsibilities, including a little fund development work.

Our first move was for our director, Shirley Pounds, and I to meet with a man named Khai, of Cornerstone Church in San Francisco. Khai worked at the San Francisco Chronicle as an account executive. He opened the door for us to make a pitch to all the account executives about helping the homeless who were only a block away.

At one time, I was once just like them—driving a nice car and making big money—I could relate well. They were my people and I was in my element. But it was Shirley who shined.

She presented the plight of those we were trying to reach in such a powerful way, that we were invited back to speak at their monthly board meeting to see what they, as an organization, could do to help the ministry. Once again, Shirley passionately promoted our cause and need.

Now it was my turn to present my well-prepared speech. I was confident and excited. I got this! But, I didn't. About three quarters through my presentation, I experienced an anxiety attack and couldn't continue.

If you've never experienced an anxiety attack before, all I can say is, it's *terrifying*. I began to feel an intense wave after wave of fear. My heart rate accelerated and my chest pounded. I had a hard time breathing. I was dizzy and my hands turned clammy, and my faced became flushed.

Was I having a heart attack?

Was I going crazy?

Was this some sort of flashback?

I tried to disguise what was happening and wrapped up the presentation with a terse "Thank you," and sat down. Shirley covered for me and addressed the crowd again, and the executives decided to give Cityteam a few thousand dollars.

We were able to purchase some food and blankets, so the presentation was a success, but I felt like a failure. I had let the ministry down.

As I walked back to the mission, I kept on wondering what had just happened. I normally have no problems with public speaking and felt so confident going in. Then, I heard that still small voice say to me, *"Apart from me, you can do nothing."* It was as clear to me as the last time I heard a voice.

After walking back to Cityteam, I went into Jonathan's office and said, "The darndest thing just happened to me..." and I went on to explain what happened during the presentation and told him about the voice I had just heard.

He said, "That's the Bible, my friend. God is speaking to you." He then opened his Bible and read John 15:5 (NIV):

> I am the vine; you are the branches. If you remain in me and I in you, you will bear much fruit; apart from me you can do nothing.

I was so amazed that what I had heard had come from the Word of God! Maybe it really *was* God who was speaking to me. My eyes were beginning to be opened to the supernatural aspect of my new faith, which was entirely new for me.

GOD WORKS IN STRANGE WAYS

Later that month a guy named Gary who'd just gotten out of the Navy, entered the program. He had recently trusted in Jesus as his Lord and Savior and approached me one evening just before dinner.

He asked me, "I was thinking about getting baptized in the ocean, what do you think?"

I told him it shouldn't be a problem and then got busy doing something else and simply forgot it.

The next morning I walked into Jonathan's office and wished him a "good morning" and then Gary came in right behind me. Before he could say anything, Jonathan looked up and saw Gary and said, "I was praying last night and the Lord told me that we should baptize Gary in the ocean."

Strange.

I turned and asked Gary if he had asked Jonathan about being baptized and before he could answer, Jonathan looked up and said, "No." I was totally blown away that Jonathan had heard God speaking to him.

Hearing voices typically falls in the category of needing psychiatric help, but this wasn't that. I'd never been a part of anything like this before. Something was happening that I couldn't rationally explain. I wondered was hearing from God simply a delusion or wishful thinking? Or maybe there is a difference between *hearing voices* and hearing *the voice of God*.

These people I was now involved with were not only living for God, but they were actually *hearing* from God as a normal part of their life! It brought me great comfort to know that God really does speak to his people, even today.

My time at Cityteam was rapidly coming to an end after only six months in the program because I was facing either jail time or home confinement—courtesy of those three DUI's. No court was going to substitute my time at the mission for time behind bars or stuck back in my hovel. I would have to face the wreckage of my past in a few weeks and pay my debt to society.

With about a week left before my court hearing, the guys were doing their usual Monday chores around the facility. Just to stay on top of things before we fed 150 or so homeless people that night, I went into the pantry. We didn't have nearly enough food.

In response to this food shortage, I did something I had never done before. I got all of the guys together and we held hands and prayed for more food and other essentials. After we prayed everyone went back to doing their chores.

The doorbell rang about thirty minutes later and I answered the door.

"Are you in charge?" the man asked.

"I'm the house manager, what do you want?"

He then proceeded to tell me that he had a truck full of all kinds of frozen food, and asked if we could take it off of his hands! I got 25 guys together and we spent the next half of an hour unloading his truck.

The new guys in the program were blown away, just the way I had been when I saw prayers being answered. One of them asked me, "Does this always happen?"

"More than you might realize..."

A WORK IN PROGRESS

All the while I was at Cityteam my attorney, Shawn, had continued to work on my behalf. For some reason he said he "believed in me." The way he continued to compassionately represent me without any financial reward helped me to grow in my faith. During my time in the ministry, I never had to appear before a judge, but now the court date was set and I'd have to face the consequences of my past actions. And I just knew I'd have to leave a ministry I had grown to love.

A few nights before my departure I got up before dinner and addressed the homeless and transient community of the TL district and told them what a pleasure it had been for me to serve them. And I really meant it. I told them how my life had changed and how sad I was to be leaving. It was an emotional time for me. For 48 years, my life was all about serving myself and *"the heck with everyone else!"*

After dinner a few of the homeless people I'd gotten to know came to thank me and even asked God to bless my life. It was then I really realized that God *had* blessed me. My new life purpose was about serving the God who made me by serving the people He loves so much. I could glorify Him by doing His will and, in turn, He blesses me with so much more than I could ever imagine!

That night I went to bed with the song "Amazing Grace" running through my head:

Amazing grace, how sweet the sound, that saved a wretch like me,

I once was lost but now am found, was blind but now I see...

A few days later I took the train from San Francisco to Gilroy and my stepbrother JR met me at the depot. He smiled as we embraced and he was really joyful at the change he saw in my life. On the way to his home we talked about life, ministry, and the future. He surprised me with some rib-eye steaks on his BBQ. It had been a long time since I had a good steak, and I'll confess, I enjoyed it immensely. But still the thought of serving time pressed in on me. Yes, my spiritual life had changed and my sin had been forgiven, but I still had to pay for my past mistakes.

After several days of freedom, I went to the Monterey County Courthouse and received my sentence: two and a half months of home confinement or two months in the county jail. Frankly, it was much better than I imagined, or *deserved*.

Home confinement it was, as long as JR didn't mind, and he didn't. I received a beautiful ankle bracelet, a home camera, and a breathalyzer. People would randomly call me three times a day and I would turn on the camera for them to watch me blow into the breathalyzer.

Soon, I was even allowed to get a job 3-4 days a week. That was a real blessing to JR and Vicki because it got me out of the house. The downside was that working at Target stocking shelves was an ego-buster for me. People I had known would come in and I could almost read their thoughts, *"Coming down in the world aren't you, Rocky?"* Clearly there were still pride issues to deal with. The upside was that the job helped me pay for all of my probationary costs such as fines, the camera, breathalyzer, and the like. And all the while I cut open boxes and filled shelves, I knew God had something else for me. I was excited about the future, even though I had no idea what to expect.

BACK TO THE FUTURE

oward the end of my probation, I sat down with JR and we talked about what might come next. I shared that maybe I should go back to Cityteam and see if I could continue to serve the homeless in some capacity. JR said I was welcome to stay with them as long as I needed and recommended for me to pray about what I should be doing. He said the Lord would let me know in my heart what to do.

A few weeks before my probation was up, I was authorized to leave for the day to attend my graduation at Cityteam Ministries. What a memorable day that was! When I arrived everyone wanted to see my ankle bracelet, and apparently I made Cityteam history as being the first person to be released from jail to speak at graduation. In that moment, my heart confirmed it—Cityteam was where I needed to serve for a while longer.

When I was called to the podium, I was overwhelmed with a deep sense of gratitude and thankfulness to the God who saved me, and who for the first time, gave me a real sense of purpose and meaning in life.

After the graduation, we attended the reception next door. It was there that Pastor Mike encouraged me to keep doing what I was doing. He said that in his twenty years of ministry, God had never let him down. Not even once.

"And Rocky," he said, "God will never let you down either."

I left the party early, because I had to be back by 6:00 p.m. My probation officer was watching me to make sure I would not violate my parole, but I was touched deeply by the event. On my return trip an overwhelming sense of joy and anticipation for the future God had planned came over me. That "joy" thing has now become a regular part of my life.

The very next day as I was riding my bike home from work along Monterey Bay. I took my hands off the handlebars, and raising them, praised God for the great things He had done in my life.

I was beginning to do all sorts of weird things I had never done before. But they didn't seem all that strange to me anymore.

My hands were raised like this for about a half-mile when I realized that all the events that had happened in my life weren't coincidences, they were *God incidences*. The Lord has His hand in my life and was reeling me in long before I realized it. As the proverbial scales were being removed from my eyes, the revelation of God's love and plan for my life grew stronger and stronger.

When I arrived home from this glorious bike ride, I told JR what God had put on my heart, just as he told me He would. I needed to go back to Cityteam in San Francisco and give back what had been so graciously given to me.

JR's response was, "I think that's great!" In human terms this decision didn't make one bit of sense, but in God's economy it was exactly what I needed to do. The Bible says to, "...seek first His Kingdom and His righteousness, and all these things will be given to you as well" (Matt 6:33). If I followed Him He'd take care of all my needs. I picked up the phone and called Trudy and my old friend Jonathan and they said that they'd have a room for me in a few days.

Going back to Cityteam was an entirely different experience than when I first arrived to enter the Drug and Alcohol Program. This time I *knew* deep down in my soul that this is where I was suppose to be.

Working in the hood, 50 or more hours a week for $500, plus room and board was not the path to success as I'd always known it. It didn't take long to realize that success in God's Kingdom does not line up with success in the world.

The trick was, before I could get hired, I had to go to the Cityteam Ministries corporate headquarters in San Jose, California, and interview for the position. It was just little old me answering a barrage of questions from twenty or so people. I felt like I was a presidential candidate for a small country.

One person on that panel was a man named Dick, who must have been in his eighties at the time. He was as sharp as a tack, very keen about recovery, and he loved the Lord Jesus.

Dick asked me about my success in the liquor business and I told him that basically, I'd been a "high class drunk." He looked at me like a dog being shown a card trick and replied, "And what is that exactly?" I got the point. He was letting me know *a drunk is a drunk, is a drunk*. Alcoholism does not discriminate by class or social status; it takes away what ever you have and destroys you.

The interview must have gone well because I was hired by Cityteam as an intern for a six-month contract. I was now the official Mission House Manager of Cityteam San Francisco, on 6th Street between Mission and Howard.

A better area for serving the homeless would be hard to find, and anyone who has been to the Tenderloin District in San Francisco knows it's Satan's playground. I began to see that a real war was being waged between the light and darkness of the world.

As the House Manager I wore several hats. This role included setting the schedule for classes, overseeing 20-30 guys in the Men's Recovery Program, and I was also given the responsibility for hospitality, which included the kitchen crew. This is the epicenter of the mission, and when trouble breaks out, it usually starts in the kitchen.

While I was in recovery, there was one crazy dude named Pedro. At one time he was a successful restaurateur in San Francisco, but he became consumed by cocaine and lost almost everything he had. While working he'd scream and throw pots and pans around the kitchen. But God got a hold of his life and he's now a dear brother in Christ and involved in international missions in Nicaragua. Where there was once anger and addiction there's now love and service.

During my internship, I learned more about myself, God, and life than I had in the previous 30 years of life trying to live it on my own. The day-to-day work of the ministry was awesome, despite the long hours. It showed me that God is real, and He's interested and active in the lives of His people. I also got to see first hand how to pray, what to pray for, and even saw specific answers to prayers.

Just one of the many ways that Cityteam taught spiritual growth was to have you mentor someone else after you've gone through the process. One day Jonathan called me into his office with my first opportunity to mentor. He wanted me to mentor a guy named Terry.

At one time, Terry had been quite successful in the business world, and chased after everything the world had to offer—money, drugs, and women (which always seem to be the top three draws for men). He found himself spending his last $150 getting into the Cityteam program in the Tenderloin.

This was a guy I could relate to. *Been there, done that.* His life had moved from Park Place to park bench—and he was as shocked as I was when I first arrived. Since I could empathize with Terry, I told Jonathan yes to mentoring him.

When I cracked open the door and saw Terry sitting there, I was reminded of my first day at the mission. Praying fervently for wisdom, I thought: *What am I going to say to this guy?* I sat down and I kid you not, it felt like Jesus was sitting right next to me—His loving arm around me, encouraging me to talk with this guy.

As Terry and I chatted, he told me about his checkered past and all the wreckage he had left behind. He just didn't see a way out of the mess he'd created. That was something I could really relate to.

When a person invests everything in material possessions and they've all been stripped away, that person feels bankrupt. I told Terry that if I was going to work with him, he would have to cooperate. He readily agreed. Desperation will do that to a person.

I could hear that still small voice in my ear as I felt the presence of God next to me saying, "Ask him if he would spend five minutes every morning in prayer, and for him to ask the God he doesn't believe in to reveal Himself to him. Then ask him to just tell Me what's on his mind."

Terry listened and agreed to do all I asked. And God started revealing himself to Terry. Keep in mind that when I first met Terry, his name and picture would have been in the dictionary after the word "atheist." His growth was slow, sometimes one step forward and two steps back, which is what often happens to so many involved in recovery.

Meanwhile, I was facing a decision. My six-month internship was nearly over. *What was I going to do with my life?* Most people advised me to take the path of least resistance, which I have discovered is not usually God's plan for a person. For me, that path would be to leave ministry and go back into the world of business.

It was my old friend and brother, Pedro, who encouraged me to seek a second internship with Cityteam. I spoke to our Director, Shirley, and she smiled and told me to pray about it. Jonathan seemed to be excited about me even entertaining the possibility of a second term.

At this point, Jonathan and I were becoming very good friends. I often sought him out for his discernment and wisdom. We prayed about where God would have me serve Him and the result was the same as before.

When the Lord lays something on your heart, it is heavy and liberating at the same time. After seeking the Lord, I believed He wanted me to apply for a second internship with Cityteam San Francisco. I was familiar with this feeling and knew that obedience was my only option. A few weeks later, I accepted a second internship for six more months.

Within a month, I heard the guy I was mentoring, Terry, had hit the wall and was upstairs packing his bags to leave the program before he graduated. Jonathan told me to go upstairs and talk to him. I went to Terry's room, knocked on his door, but there was no answer. I was afraid I might have been too late and he'd already left the mission.

Rushing back downstairs, I walked outside, and ran right into Terry. He was getting ready to walk out the gate and head toward Howard Street. We looked each other in the eye, and I'm not exactly sure what I said, but in effect I told him that nothing good had ever happened to those who left the program and walked toward Howard Street.

Somehow he was convinced to stay. He went back upstairs, unpacked his bags, and surrendered once again to the process. Terry eventually graduated and now works for two different ministries serving the Lord. We've remained great friends to this day and it is truly awesome to see the Lord working in Terry's life in such a huge way.

The lesson learned: God wants to work in all of us.

Since surrendering to our Lord and Savior Jesus Christ, my life has been profoundly changed. Not that I've been made perfect—far from it—but God is working in me to become more and more like His Son. This is an on-going process and I am so thankful for all of the people God has placed in my life to help me grow and persevere.

God has even gone beyond all I could hope for or imagine in this life and introduced me to my future helpmate I met while I was serving at Cityteam.

MEETING MY WIFE

In October of 2009, while working for Cityteam, I had an opportunity to go to a Men's Retreat for the first time at a place called Mt. Hermon in the Santa Cruz Mountains. Mt. Hermon is a huge event center; and during mealtime in the cafeteria, we ate with other people attending different retreats.

We'd just finished lunch when I offered to get the guys at our table some dessert. On the way back from the dessert bar, loaded down with brownies and cheesecake, I passed a table filled with ladies attending a Woman's Retreat from their church. I asked them if they would like some dessert. They were very kind and most of them took me up on the offer.

As I handed out plates of sweets, they asked me my name and why I offered to get them dessert. I told them it was because I was single and all the other men at my table were on their phones checking in with their wives. I didn't tell them that I was involved in ministry and had no time for the opposite sex.

What I didn't know was that my future wife, Tamara, was sitting at that very table. I didn't notice her, but apparently she noticed me. It turns out that earlier that morning, she had seen me at the local coffee shop and remembers me saying to her that I don't like "foo-foo" coffee. My now mother-in-law, Sunny, said that our future together was God-ordained.

But at that time in my life, I was too busy working on my relationship with God to get involved with a woman.

A GOOD YEAR

The next year I went to the Men's Retreat again, and guess who was giving her testimony at the Woman's Retreat that year? *Tamara.* She was there telling how God had saved her from alcohol and drug abuse ten years earlier. Her mother and she wore matching tee shirts printed with Romans 12:1-2 (ESV), the Scripture she used in her testimony:

I appeal to you therefore, brothers, by the mercies of God, to present your bodies as a living sacrifice, holy and acceptable to God, which is your spiritual worship. Do not be conformed to this world, but be transformed by the renewal of your mind, that by testing you may discern what is the will of God, what is good and acceptable and perfect.

For ten years she'd been getting her life back together. She'd been raising two boys and working as a Cosmetology instructor, and at last she was thinking she might be ready to settle down again.

Tamara had told Sunny a couple of months before the retreat that, "If God wants to bring a Christian man into my life, I'm ready." They laughed together, and joked about the man they met the year before—which was *me*!

As they drove up to the Post Office at Mt. Hermon that year, Tamara said that if she saw me again this year, that she would talk to me. Her mom said that if God really wanted us together, He could have me walk right in front of the car. And *I did*. No joke. This was exactly what happened! But instead of talking to me then, Tamara told her mom she was there to give her testimony first—not find a husband.

During a lunch break, I was talking with friends when I looked over and recognized the same women who I brought desserts to the year before. They were too busy listening to a worship band to notice me.

"Hi, are you the same ladies I met last year and brought desserts to?"

They looked me over and then a smile of recognition lit up on their faces, "Yes" they replied, almost in unison. We all laughed.

Soon our conversation turned to the Lord, worship music, and my work with Cityteam in San Francisco, serving recovering drug addicts and the homeless. One of the gals, told me her husband, Don, liked to help the poor and less fortunate. She asked me for my phone number so he could call me if he was interested in helping.

Tamara was standing closest to me, so I put my number in her phone and got her number as well. I told them that they had my number and for Don to give me a call. One of them said, not loud enough for Tamara to hear, that I had Tamara's number too, and to call her. That lady went on to tell me what a nice and godly lady Tamara was (and still is).

Intrigued, I texted her while they were having lunch and she actually replied. We started texting quite a bit and I eventually invited her to go to Cornerstone Church in San Francisco with me. Eventually I went with her to her church, North Creek

Church, in Walnut Creek. We really were enjoying each other's company.

On her birthday, I asked her to come and spend the day with me in San Francisco. We walked all over the city, not wanting to end our time together. And we both had the blisters on our feet to prove it!

I told the Cityteam leaders that I was ready to get married again and they warned me what my role as a godly husband would look like. *Yikes.* I'm to love her as Jesus sacrificially loved the church? That's a big order to fill. But, with God's power I could be the husband He would want me to be.

So, I proposed on her birthday in front of Cornerstone Church and she accepted, saying she trusted that the Lord would bring the right man in His timing. We were married a year later in October of 2011 in Sunny's backyard.

At that point, I ended my internship with Cityteam and needed to find a job. I was not only a new husband, but was also a father to Tamara's two sons, Jesse and Dillon.

I look back at my life and see how I had lost a son when Nerea took him to Mexico, and now, I had two sons! God continued to amaze me and gave me more than anything I could imagine.

Little did I know then, but my job search would take us back to Colorado.

LIFE NOW

If you had shown me a snapshot in 2009 of what my life would look like in 2015 when we moved back to Colorado, I would've told you that *you* were high and using drugs. In my mind, the life I now have would've been impossible to attain. I can only attribute my redemption to one thing: God, Jesus, and the Holy Spirit—our triune God.

I was lost and now am found.

Everyone, myself included, are sinners by nature and by choice. Sin separates us from God. He's holy. We're not. Holiness and sin are incompatible.

God paid the penalty sin deserves, separation from God, by sending His Son to pay the penalty for us!

That's why Christ was crucified.

The Good News is that He didn't stay dead.

Those who trust that Jesus died for their sins are restored in relationship with the Father and it is all done by His grace.

And when we die, we will live with God instead of separated from Him.

In the meantime, we start the process of being transformed into Christ's likeness. That just means I die to my selfishness and become filled with His Spirit so I can now live for Him.

Pretty simple, huh?

As I reflect back on my life and this journey, there was something that I was always missing, and that something was Jesus Christ! He is the great fisher of men. He set the hook in me before I even knew it. And, He let me run with the line to accommodate my self-will. But, when the time was right, He yanked on the line to draw me a little closer to Him. Then, He slowly reeled me in. Because of His goodness, He gave me a life I never imagined I'd have.

After Tamara and I were married, I was offered a sales position with a company in Fort Collins, Colorado. I jumped at the chance and moved with Tamara and our son Jesse. We eventually bought a house that we've opened to all who are in need. It's Tamara's first home *ever*.

Jesus has taken my mess and made it His message.

My journey may be foreign to you or maybe you can relate in some way. I am no longer the same person I once was. Something happened to me that was—there's no other way to say it—supernatural in nature.

Every day is a new adventure.

Every day I put into practice everything I learned at Cityteam San Francisco.

Every day I pray and freely talk to the Creator of the whole universe. *This* is my new reality.

Currently, I serve the homeless in Northern Colorado. I'm involved in an evangelical church and study the Word. I'm using my gifts to build up the body of Christ—the church—and reaching out to those caught up in drug and alcohol abuse.

Life is great, but not without its challenges.

Once I got saved and trusted in Jesus Christ as my Lord and Savior, I became painfully aware that I had three real and powerful enemies: the world, the flesh (that is, my own sin nature), and Satan (including his minions). But greater is He that is in me, than he that is in this world.

Our Lord and Savior Jesus Christ hasn't left us defenseless in this battle. God has given us spiritual battle gear we are to put on every day, and He has given us His Body, the church, where we are encouraged and discipled for ministry.

I'm so thankful to God for giving me my beautiful wife, Tamara. She became a Christian some eight years before I did and she has been clean and sober for that entire time. Tamara continues to inspire me and Tamara has also shared her sons, Jesse and Dillon with me. God willing, I'll be reconciled to my son Andoni some day, who still resides in Mexico City.

FINAL THOUGHTS

May I encourage you, if you are struggling with any kind of addiction or past pain, to seek the Lord Jesus Christ. He *will* break the chains that bind you. To those who are broken and don't know where to turn, I pray this little story of my life will show you the way to eternal peace and joy in Christ and that you will gain a spark of hope that real change is possible..

My life verse has become Proverbs 3:5-6 (ESV): "Trust in the Lord with all your heart and do not lean on your own understanding. In all your ways acknowledge Him, and He will make your path straight." Trusting in God is not a panacea for all our problems—in fact, once you become a Christian you may face more challenges than you ever have in the past—but God will give you the strength to endure.

Jesus said in Matthew 11:28, "Come to me, all you who are weary and burdened, and I will give you rest." And He will! If any of you who are reading this are struggling with addiction or a serious stronghold in your life that you cannot seem to break free from, may I encourage you to look for help in a non-profit Christian-based recovery program. In 2009 I had no clue there were free programs out there that not only deal with the physical issue of addiction, but the spiritual dimension as well.

As I reflect on my past and try to make sense of it all, I can honestly say that everything I've ever learned in this life that had any meaning and substance has come through afflictions. So don't think that your current pain is a waste. Christ is a redeemer. He can redeem your life, your pain, and your mess. I had to hit rock bottom before God got my attention and began His transformation process in me. Now, I'm all ears and daily thanking Him for my sobriety and my salvation.

My prayer is that some of you won't wait as long as I did before you understand that there is a God who loves you. A God who offers purpose and meaning in life that transcends every worldly offer of success.

For most of my life I was utterly lost to one addiction or another, but both my story, and my Savior, prove that *what is lost can be found.*

DISCUSSION QUESTIONS FOR ROCK BOTTOM

1. Rocky shares many sides of his personality before his fall into addiction, during, and after. What did you admire, cringe at, or detest?

2. Has this book changed how you look at an addict? Why or why not?

3. Rocky's childhood included elements of child abuse, abandonment, isolation, estrangement from a parent, divorce, neglect, and addiction. What role do you think those experiences played in his adulthood?

4. What was the triggering event that had him make the jump from alcoholism to opioid abuse and full-blown heroin addiction?

5. What part of this book inspired you in some way? Explain.

6. What is a life lesson, or two, that can be learned from Rocky's story?

7. Do any of the issues he experienced affect your life? How so —directly, on a daily basis, or more generally?

8. What solutions does Rocky propose as aids to recovery from addiction? Do you agree or do you have alternate ideas about what is necessary for recovery?

9. Do you think there needs to be a faith component to recovery programs? Explain.

10. After having read the book, what's one thing you learned and one thing you want to learn more about?

TRIBUTE TO THE FALLEN SOLDIERS OF ADDICTION

Maurice Jerome

Glen Bartlett

John Medow

Doug Schweiker

Peter Marchand

Marty Barrego

Gregory Wright

Raja Moler

Nate Pegis

Grant Ballard

Cary Smith

Steve Malloy

Sally Merritt

SPECIAL THANKS

Dr. Doug Kher – Co-Writer, Friend & Senior Pastor Cornerstone Church, Johnstown, CO

Mikal Keefer – Friend

Danny Dodge – Photographer

Shirley & Mike Pounds – My Spiritual Parents, Restore Ministry

Paul Chan – Mentor and Pastor

Jonathan Zingkhai – Recovery Manager & Mentor of Cityteam, San Francisco

Mike Moberg – Senior Pastor, Outpost Church, San Francisco

Randy Rupley & Peter Marchand – House Managers, Cityteam, San Francisco

Trudy Read – Cityteam, San Francisco

Michael Cartwright – Evangelist

ABOUT THE AUTHOR

During my recovery, and after, I worked alongside the amazing people of Cityteam, San Francisco for over three years and was privileged to invest in the homeless community for the sake of the Gospel.

When the Lord blessed my life with a new family—my wife and children—we moved back to Colorado and I have since been involved in loving on the homeless in Northern Colorado and reaching out to any and all who struggle with addiction.

In fact, a portion of the proceeds from the sale of this book will go to help those recovering from drug and alcohol addiction. If you are interested in buying the book in bulk, please contact me.

Because mine is a story of hope, I am happy to share it with schools, youth groups, churches, recovery groups, and more. If you are interested in having me come and speak, please connect with me in one of the following ways:

Rocky Romano

rockyrre@gmail.com

www.rockyaromano.com

If you're still interested in my story, you can watch an interview I did on YouTube[(r)] called the *Heroin Addict Next Door.*

If after reading my story, you want to share yours with me, please do!